SH*T
MOMENTS
IN NEW
ZEALAND
SPORT

'New Zealand rules' was a short-lived and unpopular sport.

SH*T MOMENTS IN NEW ZEALAND SPORT

RICK FURPHY AND GEOFF RISSOLE

ALLEN&UNWIN

SYDNEY · MELBOURNE · AUCKLAND · LONDON

CONTENTS

INTRODUCTION

New Zealand isn't good at many sports. We only really play the English ones, and we only excel at ones that involve either beating people up (rugby) or sitting on our arses (sailing, rowing, equestrian, cycling).

The main one, of course, is rugby. The fifteen-man code is our national religion and the All Blacks are our gods. Any time the ABs don't smash their opponents by at least 75 points is a national day of mourning. In truth, this book could have been just All Blacks losses—and the ABs' darkest days are included in this volume.

But there are numerous other sporting mishaps and humiliations that have befallen our fair nation, from epic chokes on the world stage, to refereeing injustices, to shameless off-field shenanigans. Some have been the subject of endless hours of talkback radio and vats of newspaper ink, while others have managed to fly under the radar.

All the events in this volume have been ranked according to an exacting set of criteria developed by the Centre for Sporting Despair at the prestigious University of Matamata. These criteria allow us to determine the precise shitness of a particular moment in New Zealand sport, using a 57-point turdometer that includes such questions as: Did the All Blacks lose? Was it a World Cup? Was Australia involved?

Sport is part of the fabric of our nation. It's not just how we spend the majority of our free time and also most of our work time—it's the core of our fragile national identity. Unfortunately, as every sports fan knows, it's also a largely punishing pastime. Losing a week's rent and our temper over a grown man playing a child's game. Idolising someone with superhuman athleticism and caring more about their achievements than most people in our immediate family. Throwing around the phrase 'per capita' a lot during the Olympics. The great Kiwi tradition of finding a scapegoat. Sport possesses the wonderful ability to break your heart and take a dump on it in one swift movement. We can't live with it, but we can't live without it.

So, for everyone out there cursed with the sports bug, we hope you find some catharsis in this light-hearted shortlist of shit, this comprehensive catalogue of catastrophes, this dossier of diabolical debacles and downright disasters. And remember: the only thing worse than sport are the people who think they are too good to care about it.

Professional boxing had no age limits until 1927.

TIMELINE:
A HISTORY OF HUMILIATION

4 BILLION BC   Māui defeats the Sun in a heavyweight bout to create the 24-hour day, making us all work more and sleep less (see page 37).

1850   First game of 'New Zealand Rules' is played in Mosgiel. The game fails to take off because it is basically 'rugby but blind drunk'.

1905   Referee refuses to award Bob Deans' try against Wales, spoiling the Original All Blacks' undefeated Northern Hemisphere tour (see page 88).

1915   New Zealand competitive hill-climbing team receives a sound thrashing from Turkish home team (see page 71).

1916   All Blacks squad dies in the *Titanic* disaster, making a mockery of pre-tour nickname 'The Unsinkables'.

1927   Sheepdog trials are invented as a means of keeping score in Southland's competitive bestiality scene.

1928   Australia steals champion horse Phar Lap (see page 58).

1954   The Wairarapa Bush rugby team survives a plane crash in the Urewera by resorting to cannibalism (see page 64).

1955   New Zealand cricket team bowled out for 26 against England, setting the record for the lowest-ever total in test cricket (see page 90).

1960	All Blacks send all-white team on tour of South Africa to appease racists (see page 100).
1961	Arthur Lydiard invents slow running, AKA jogging (see page 23).
1963	Kiwis lose to South Africa at Carlaw Park despite South Africa not playing league (see page 70).
1967	National deity Colin Meads gets sent off against Scotland (see page 38).
1970	Sylvia Potts trips metres from finish line at the Edinburgh Commonwealth Games (see page 87).
1972	Keith Murdoch gets sent home from All Blacks tour after security-guard scuffle (see page 40).
1972	The lawn bowls community is rocked after three-time national champion Bjorn Gundersen tests positive for steroids. Lawn bowls wouldn't be this adversely affected by a chemical again until the invention of Viagra.
1973	Rodney Redmond scores a century on debut but never plays another test for New Zealand (see page 55).
1980	New Zealand win zero medals at the Moscow Olympics (see page 96).
1981	Australia bowl underarm against New Zealand, in a disgusting display of unsportsmanship (see page 114).

Early biathlons consisted of a combined cycling and wedgie event.

Hugging was a popular spectator sport in the early 20th century.

Weightlifting was invented several years before barbells, forcing early competitors to improvise.

1994	Three young Black Caps are hung out to dry for puffing a bit of weed on tour (see page 94).
1995	The New Zealand public develops an unhealthy but thankfully short-lived obsession with red socks (and yachting).
1995	Suzie the waitress costs the All Blacks the Rugby World Cup (see page 110).
1995	Auckland Warriors make their debut (see page 41).
1996	Martin Crowe invents Cricket Max (see page 35).
1996	The America's Cup gets a hiding from a Māori activist (see page 43).
1999	Football Kingz make their NSL debut (see page 78).
1999	Silver Ferns choke in the Netball World Cup final against Australia (see page 102).
1999	All Blacks lose the Rugby World Cup semi-final to France (see page 77).
2000	Kiwis smashed 52–0 by Kangaroos in Anzac test.
2000	David Tua blows heavyweight title shot in Lennox Lewis blowout.
2002	Future PM and two-time election loser Bill English takes part in a charity boxing bout against 'the Psychlone'. The much-hyped mystery opponent turns out to be some bloke he went to uni with, setting the correct level of disappointment for an event involving Bill English.

2002	Warriors lose their first grand final (see page 68).
2003	All Blacks lose the Rugby World Cup semi-final to Australia (see page 66).
2003	Russell Coutts and Brad Butterworth win the America's Cup for Alinghi (see page 81).
2005	All Black Andrew Hore fails to qualify for the Olympics in Marine Mammal Sharpshooting (see page 44).
2006	All Black Jerry Collins urinates on the pitch before a match (see page 31).
2006	Ranfurly Shield is devalued by being won by North Harbour (see page 28).
2006	New Zealand Knights kicked out of the A-League (see page 78).
2007	Former Tall Black Brendon Pongia repeatedly farts on *Good Morning*.
2007	All Blacks flop out of the Rugby World Cup in the quarters (see page 106).
2009	Kiwis smashed 58–0 by Kangaroos in centenary test.
2009	Chiefs suffer biggest-ever Super Rugby grand final loss (see page 62).
2010	All Whites draw every game at 2010 World Cup (see page 24).

The Tour de Taranaki was a particularly difficult course.

2011	PM John Key has awkward three-way handshake on live TV (see page 21).
2012	Shot-putter Nadzeya Ostapchuk cheats New Zealand's Valerie Adams out of Olympic gold (see page 103).
2013	Team New Zealand blow 7–0 lead in America's Cup (see page 113).
2014	Jack Bauer denied Tour de France stage win at the death (see page 60).
2017	Kiwis lose Rugby League World Cup semi-final to Fiji (see page 98).
2018	Silver Ferns finish a lowly fourth at the Commonwealth Games (see page 53).
2019	Black Caps 'lose' Cricket World Cup final (see page 119).
2019	All Blacks lose Rugby World Cup semi-final to England (see page 52).
2020	The sporting world is thrown into chaos due to the COVID-19 pandemic.
2022	Former Tall Black Brendon Pongia projectile-vomits all over Hilary Barry on *Seven Sharp*.
2023	The Melbourne Cup is cancelled due to concerns over animal welfare, and replaced by a Vegan Penny Farthing Marathon where the winner is judged on the quality of their moustache and their ska band's demo tape.

2025   Controversy as the Mongrel Mob enters a syndicate in the America's Cup.

2027   Former Tall Black Brendon Pongia shits his pants on *Dancing with the Stars*.

2028   E-sports are included in the Olympics for the first time; the subsequent wave of boomer outrage is so great that the entire country's communication network is taken offline as every male over the age of 65 tries to ring talkback at once.

2036   Bullrush is added as an exhibition sport for the Tauranga Olympics, resulting in New Zealand's only gold medal of the games.

2042   Prime Minister Max Key outlaws cycling.

2086   NZ win their first FIFA World Cup, a victory largely marred by the fact the majority of the globe has been rendered uninhabitable for humans and their main competition was a team of genetically-modified penguins representing Antarctica.

2769   The All Blacks' 766-year Bledisloe Cup-winning run comes to an end.

2920   New Zealand loses the Boganfights World Cup final to Australia.

2999   All sport is permanently banned by new Earth president Seriousbot-3000.

50: John Key's awkward three-way

'In amongst this fantastic moment of Richie holding the World Cup, I thought to myself, you know, I reckon I'm going to see that again.'—John Key, NZ Prime Minister

WHAT HAPPENED: Rugby World Cup final, 2011. The All Blacks had just pulled off a nail-biting 8–7 victory over France to win the Webb Ellis Cup for the second time, slaying New Zealand's collective fears that the ABs would never win another World Cup again. Moments after the trophy was presented to Richie McCaw on the Eden Park turf, New Zealand Prime Minister John Key and International Rugby Board chairman Bernard Lapasset both shook the All Blacks captain's hand at the same time.

Replays show that Key lunged first. Quick as a flash, Lapasset, standing between the two, hijacked the handshake, leaving Key fumbling with a couple of McCaw's fingers. Despite being about as welcome as Brian Tamaki on Grindr, the ham-fisted PM was already committed, and desperately clutched the hand sandwich until the Frenchman let go. The farcical scene was broadcast live into millions of homes around the world.

WHY IT'S SHIT: There's nothing worse than an interloper in a threesome. What should have been the greatest photo opportunity of John Key's career, just before an election—and a moment to savour for national hero McCaw—instead devolved into a scene of pure pisstake destined to be immortalised as a GIF. Somehow, the Prime Minister of New Zealand, the world champion All Blacks captain and some French guy had managed to concoct the most awkward three-way since Harry, Ron and Hermione got trashed on butterbeer at Magical Mardi Gras.

49: Arthur Lydiard invents jogging

WHAT HAPPENED: Famous coach Arthur Lydiard made his name training legendary middle-distance runners Peter Snell and Murray Halberg with excruciating marathon runs through the Waitakeres. His innovative training regime ensured his athletes peaked for their most important races and resulted in a bounty of medals at the 1960 and 1964 Olympics, including double gold for Snell in Tokyo. Lydiard later popularised his patented method of running nowhere in particular for extended periods of time by rebranding it as an exercise activity for the masses.

WHY IT'S SHIT: Jogging, which sounds more like Scandinavian slang for some sort of sub-zero cottaging than an exercise activity, is beloved by wankers the world over. One of the most boring activities known to man and enjoyed only by the terminally dull who can endure the stultifying boredom of running slowly for ages, the punishing pastime was basically the crossfit of the 1970s. If it weren't for Lydiard then running would probably have been reserved for appropriate times only: when something is on fire, when you have a turtlehead poking out or when her husband comes home early. Next time you are cornered by your ruddy-faced manager blagging on about how he is training for a half marathon, just remember you have Arthur Lydiard to thank.

48: All Whites' draw-fest

WHAT HAPPENED: In 2010, after the All Whites scraped into the FIFA World Cup for just the second time courtesy of a fortuitous 1–0 aggregate win over the international powerhouse of Bahrain, most fans would probably have been happy to see them return from South Africa with a single point. Instead, they showed they were capable of competing on the world stage—not by actually winning any games, but by drawing with teams that did.

The unfancied All Whites earned their first draw of the tournament with a last-gasp Winston Reid equaliser against Slovakia in their opening match. They followed this up with a draw with world champions Italy, after Daniele De Rossi's Oscar-worthy tumble earned the Azzurri a penalty to cruelly cancel out Shane Smeltz's opener. The All Whites then wrapped up their round robin with a goalless stalemate against Paraguay, ending their tournament with a whimper as their nation had expected, when a single goal would have seen them progress. Without winning a game, the All Whites returned to a heroes' welcome, a parade and a handful of Halberg Awards. There was even a celebratory DVD entitled *Undefeated: The All Whites' World Cup Story*, which is a bit like releasing a porn compilation with all the cum shots edited out.

WHY IT'S SHIT: If a draw is like kissing your sister, then this World Cup was like an Invercargill after-ball. Finishing as the tournament's only unbeaten team, and yet exiting at the first hurdle, was a frustrating paradox that left an entire country confused about whether we should have been proud of the All Whites or lamenting their inability to fulfil the potential we never knew they had. It would have all been much simpler if they had just lost all their games like they were supposed to. The All Whites rectified this dilemma by promptly returning to shit again once the World Cup was over.

New Zealanders are inherently suspicious of football given its preponderance of fancy Europeans and absolute dearth of crushing violence, but the fact we are generally rubbish at it doesn't help either.

47: Dennis Conner's TV tanty

WHAT HAPPENED: Four-time America's Cup winner Dennis Conner had already earned a reputation among the Kiwi public as 'Dirty Den', after he accused the New Zealand team of cheating by building *KZ7* out of fibreglass rather than aluminium. He followed this up by winning the 1988 America's Cup with a catamaran under a liberal interpretation of the rules and calling Kiwi skipper David Barnes a loser. Incredibly, Dirty Den strolled into a trap of his own making when he agreed to appear on New Zealand television in 1989 to promote some dumb boat-themed board game. Agitator par excellence Paul Holmes inaugurated the first episode of his new current-affairs show *Holmes* by ambushing Conner, pressing him to apologise for cheating in the 1988 America's Cup. The fiery confrontation culminated with a teary-eyed Conner storming off the set, in an iconic moment in New Zealand television history.

WHY IT'S SHIT: Most Kiwis were surprised that anybody could get that worked up about boats. The Cheeky Yankee's tanty confirmed most New Zealanders' scepticism about the America's Cup—a sporting contest decided in a court of law isn't much of a sporting contest at all. The intense interview also cemented both Holmes' reputation as a controversial broadcaster, and Conner's as a New Zealand sporting villain.

46: Richard Loe's low blow

WHAT HAPPENED: For reasons still unknown, Richard Loe, during the 1992 NPC final between Waikato and Otago, decided to try to pop All Blacks teammate Greg Cooper's eyeball out of its socket. Loe had form when it came to on-field acts of barbarity—this incident was shortly after he had chosen to congratulate Wallabies winger Paul Carozza's try-scoring efforts with an elbow drop, smearing his nose across his face.

WHY IT'S SHIT: Although rugby nominally seems like the sort of game designed by Vikings on their day off from pillaging and setting fire to clergy, it actually prides itself on a well-honed sense of mateship and fair play. Blatant acts of thuggery like Loe trying to alleviate Cooper of his eyeball tend to show the lie behind such assumptions. All Blacks fans like to think that their lads are above such brutish acts—it's a bit of a blow when they are presented with incontrovertible evidence that sometimes the chaps in black are capable of being pricks as well.

For his trouble, Loe received a six-month suspension, and later channelled his controversial nature into a career as a talkback radio host.

45: Harbour sully the Shield

'I know we can be a hard team to support at times, but thanks for sticking with us.'—Rua Tipoki, North Harbour captain

WHAT HAPPENED: The Ranfurly Shield is one of New Zealand rugby's great prizes, its glorious history filled with the sort of white-knuckled tussles and Herculean efforts that will bring a tear to the eye of even the ruddiest old tighthead. Auckland defeating Canterbury in 1985's 'Match of the Century'. Auckland's epic undefeated streak of the '80s and '90s. Something called 'Manuwhenua' winning it in 1927. Conversely, North Harbour is the country's youngest union, formed only in 1985, and has put in three decades of spectacular mediocrity, failing to achieve much of anything aside from ending Jeff Wilson's coaching career. North Harbour is most famous for its involvement in the 'Battle of the Bridge', a rivalry with Auckland of which the high point was the cool nickname. North Harbour had previously unsuccessfully challenged for the Ranfurly Shield ten times, including 1996 when Harbour recorded three futile attempts in a single season. Given its glorious history, it's hard to deny that the Log o' Wood lost a considerable amount of its lustre when it was claimed by the flakiest union in the country following Harbour's 21–17 victory over Canterbury in 2006.

WHY IT'S SHIT: The result stunned the rugby world in much the same way as somebody might be surprised when they try to squeak out a silent fart in a crowded elevator and end up with a trouser load of pants pudding. It seemed unthinkable that the one union with as little history as North Harbour could ever claim a prize as vaunted at the Ranfurly Shield, a development that somehow diminished both in the process.

The victory parade was attended by a sparse smattering of yoga mums and personal trainers, a sharp contrast to the sort of celebrations usually enjoyed by Ranfurly Shield winners that have actual fans. Fortunately, North Harbour eventually realised their utter unworthiness, and lost the Shield to Waikato 55-7 in one of the most callow defences in Ranfurly Shield history. For the most part the New Zealand rugby public have made vow to basically ignore the whole embarrassing debacle and, much like that time Jamie Macintosh played for the All Blacks, pretend like it never happened.

44: O for Orsum

'I'd like to buy a vowel. P.'—David Tua, boxer

WHAT HAPPENED: Olympic boxer and future heavyweight contender David Tua created New Zealand television history in 1992 when he took part in a celebrity episode of *Wheel of Fortune*. Tua proceeded to wage a one-man war on literacy when he made his now-famous letter request: 'O for awesome!' The boxer later followed this up by requesting to buy a vowel—a 'P'. The home viewer who Tua was playing for ended up winning the consolation prize of a pen.

WHY IT'S SHIT: While nobody should expect someone who gets punched in the head for a living to be a master of the English language, Tua's chaotic *Wheel of Fortune* appearance provided a classic New Zealand television moment up there with that time Thingee's eye exploded, Angela D'Audney getting her tits out and Selwyn Toogood's sex tape.[1] Tua would later go on to have a decorated boxing career, culminating in a championship bout with Lennox Lewis. While he was unsuccessful in wresting the belt off Lewis, this was down to his diminutive stature and lack of reach rather than his lack of facility with the English language.

---

1   The sex tape was later leaked online under the title *It's in My Ballbag!*

43: Jerry Collins irrigates the pitch

'He did his best to hide it. It'd be really good if we didn't make a big issue of it.'—Steve Hansen, All Blacks coach

WHAT HAPPENED: A few moments prior to the kick-off of a 2006 Tri-Nations game against Australia at the late, lamented Lancaster Park, All Black Jerry Collins knelt down like he was about to deliver an inspirational speech in an American sports film, before sliding what could only be a brown anaconda out the bottom of his shorts and irrigating the pitch with a generous spray.

WHY IT'S SHIT: Unfortunately, this will always be remembered as the day a generation of Kiwi men found out they didn't measure up to an All Black in more ways than one. Collins became part of the pantheon of sporting greats who found themselves caught short on the field of play: John Daly filling a nappy at Augusta, Yvette Williams dropping a deuce while landing a world-record attempt at the 1954 Vancouver Commonwealth Games, and the entire 1986 New Zealand cricket team fouling their whites the now iconic shade of beige after being beset by a particularly savage case of Delhi belly.

TOP 10
WORST TEAM NAMES IN NZ SPORT

1. **BAY OF PLENTY STEAMERS** (Rugby Union, Mitre 10 Cup)—Slang for a massive dump, which accurately sums up the performance of the average BOP rugby team.

2. **THAMES VALLEY SWAMP FOXES** (Rugby Union, Heartland Championship)—There are no foxes in Thames Valley, but there is a swamp.

3. **HAWKE'S BAY UNICORNS** (Rugby League, Lion Red Cup)—There are no unicorns in Hastings.

4. **WAIRARAPA BUSH** (Rugby Union, Heartland Championship)—Masterton's love of pubes is an odd thing to celebrate in their team name.

5. **COUNTIES MANUKAU COMETZ** (Netball, National Bank Cup)—The only thing the region has to do with a comet is that it would be improved by being hit by one. Extra points for the 'Z'.

6. **TARANAKI MOUNTAINAIRS** (Basketball, NBL)—Very non-threatening for a team name. Sounds like an air freshener.

7. **CHRISTCHURCH CITY SHINERS** (Rugby League, Lion Red Cup)—A shiner is a black eye, something that no professional sports team should be proud of.

8. **BLACK COCKS** (Badminton)—While only short-lived, the nickname for the national badminton team did provide some interesting internet search mishaps.

9. **HURRICANES** (Rugby Union, Super Rugby)—Naming your team after a weather phenomenon in the opposite hemisphere is the height of stupidity.

10. **ALL BLACKS** (Rugby Union)—A misleading name that is certain to confuse the average American about the level of blatant racism in New Zealand.

A typical Cricket Max crowd.

42: Cricket . . . to the Max!

'At some grounds it was a better idea to introduce all the spectators to all the players.'—Don Cameron, sports journalist

WHAT HAPPENED: If Martin Crowe was a cricketing genius, then Cricket Max was like that time Michael Jordan tried to play baseball. While Crowe cannily recognised the entertainment potential of a condensed version of the game, he also managed to overcomplicate it with a number of esoteric rules that rendered it incomprehensible to all but the most dedicated of supporters.

Launched in 1996, the initial version of Cricket Max featured two innings of ten overs each (mirroring test cricket), 'The Max Zone' (a vaguely erotic-sounding concept designed to reward batsmen for playing through the V by giving them double runs), and ruling out the ability to be caught if the ball was hit straight down the ground. The game even featured a fourth stump and no LBWs. It seemed like the sort of sport that might have been conceived after a long month on the peyote while watching marathon reruns of the 1992 Cricket World Cup (which may or may not have been the case).

WHY IT'S SHIT: Like eating kale, voting for the ACT party or preventing climate change, Cricket Max was an ambitious endeavour that ultimately failed to capture the imagination of the public. While it enjoyed a brief period of popularity and even included some Cricket Max internationals against befuddled touring teams shanghaied into taking part, Cricket Max was eventually supplanted by the far more popular (and far less convoluted) T20.

The success of T20 shows that Crowe had the right idea overall—he was just ahead of his time and over-egged the pudding to an almost comical degree. Cricket Max is waiting for an ironic hipster revival, re-creating the days when you could blast a straight drive through the Max Zone for 12!

41: Māui KOs the Sun

WHAT HAPPENED: After being forced to eat cold hāngī in the dark, Māui hatched a plan to slow the Sun's rapid pace: he would challenge the impatient celestial body to a heavyweight clash to determine the proper length of the day. In an ambush akin to Douglas vs Tyson, the demigod delivered a thunderous KO that knocked the Sun senseless, putting the celestial body on the canvas in a record 13 seconds.

WHY IT'S SHIT: While it's undoubtedly one of Aotearoa's first big sporting upsets, it's hard to understate the fallout caused by Māui's epic knockout. This defeat is directly responsible for the 40-hour work week and New Zealand's appalling rate of skin cancer—if he had left the Sun to its hasty transit then we'd all be enjoying four-hour work weeks and the skin complexion of an albino newborn.

Māui had previously dabbled in sporting infamy when he blitzed the field at a fishing competition by reeling in the North Island, only to be stripped of the title when it was revealed he had used a non-regulation rod made from his grandmother's jawbone.

40: Colin Meads sees red

'For one with Meads' world-wide reputation for robust play, this was rather like sending a burglar to prison for a parking offence.'—The Daily Telegraph

WHAT HAPPENED: In 1967, legendary All Black Colin Meads was sent off during a test match at Murrayfield for trying to kick a ball loose and copping the Scottish first-five David Chisholm square in the chest. In an era before ubiquitous cameras and video referees sticking in their noses mid-game, such violent acts were far from uncommon. Indeed, many players of Meads' ilk were employed for their ability to turn opposing playmakers into human pretzels first and their ability to actually play the game second. Still, All Blacks fans bristled at the suggestion that St Colin would be sent from the field for the relatively trivial offence of nearly booting a man's head clean off his body.

WHY IT'S SHIT: Colin Meads is basically New Zealand rugby's version of Jesus, so sending him off was sacrilegious. This rabid veneration tends to overlook the fact that Colin Meads attacked the field like Prince Tui Teka attacking a buffet. Deploying a raw-boned aggression that bordered on outright violence, if Meads were a Springbok he would have haunted the nightmares of Kiwi kids for generations, but because he was 'one of ours', they built a statue of him in Te Kuiti.

Colin Meads combined matinee idol looks with the cold dead eyes of a killer.

39: Keith Murdoch's marching orders

'If I faced exactly the same situation again I would make exactly the same decision.'—Ernie Todd, All Blacks tour manager

WHAT HAPPENED: After defeating Wales 19–16 at Cardiff Arms Park in 1972, All Blacks hardman Keith Murdoch became involved in a confrontation with security guard Peter Grant at the Angel Hotel. Sanctioned for his role in the altercation, Murdoch was immediately dispatched back to New Zealand in disgrace. On the way home, Murdoch jumped off the plane in Australia and disappeared into the Outback like a cross between D.B. Cooper and Bigfoot.

WHY IT'S SHIT: Murdoch's dismissal is an iconic episode in the storied history of the All Blacks, a rare occasion where a team that prides itself on discipline and preserving its illustrious legacy was faced with a threat to its reputation from a wayward team member. While it was a massive event in the history of the All Blacks, it seems almost quaint in terms of modern sporting scandals. In a day and age where someone can plead guilty to assaulting their partner and then represent the All Blacks at the World Cup the following year, it's hard to believe Murdoch's transgressions would even rate much of a mention.

Murdoch lived out his days in anonymity in the Australian Outback, eschewing most attempts by the media to make contact.

38: The Warriors' disappointing debut

'Lets gone Warriors.'—Famous fan banner

WHAT HAPPENED: In a shocking development from which the New Zealand sporting landscape has yet to fully recover, the Auckland Warriors debuted in the NSWRL in 1995. As the first New Zealand team to participate in an Australian professional sporting competition, the Warriors' debut was accompanied by the sort of expectation and fanfare usually reserved for when KFC figures out a new thing to do to chicken. The Warriors narrowly missed the finals in their inaugural season after being docked two competition points for an interchange error. Two decades later, the Warriors are still yet to live up to that early anticipation, recording a paltry eight finals appearances and zero titles.

WHY IT'S SHIT: It would be six seasons, two collapsed competitions and a salary-cap breach before the Warriors eventually made the finals. Despite reaching two grand finals, the Warriors are still yet to notch up their first premiership—something that doesn't seem likely in the immediate or even not-so-immediate future. Warriors fans have had to make do with an exciting brand of ad-lib football, a handful of homegrown heroes and more alternate jerseys than you can shake a can of Woodstock at.

37: America's Cup gets a hiding

'We heard we are going to be racing for the America's Plate now.'—Brad Butterworth, Team New Zealand tactician

WHAT HAPPENED: One year earlier, New Zealand was awash with America's Cup hysteria—Peter Blake was a national hero, everyone had a pair of red socks and New Zealand had been able to plug the hole in our gaping national self-esteem with a shiny trophy in a sport that we had previously given zero fucks about.

On 14 March 1996, Māori sovereignty activist Benjamin Peri Nathan marched into Auckland's Royal New Zealand Yacht Squadron clubrooms and smashed the glass cabinet containing the famous trophy. Fifty whacks with a sledgehammer later, the Auld Mug resembled an empty tinnie that had been stood on by a Pressie's tighthead.

WHY IT'S SHIT: Aotearoa just can't have nice things. The America's Cup had only been out of its home country once before in its 145-year history. While this incident was quite embarrassing in an international sense, there is something undeniably funny about a trophy awarded to the winner of a multimillion-dollar yacht race being smashed into oblivion with a sledgehammer. Tu meke.

36: Andrew Hore's pot shot

'A grossly irresponsible, spontaneous act of hooliganism.'—Judge Peter Rollo

WHAT HAPPENED: Previously best known for having the most position-appropriate surname in rugby, former All Blacks and Hurricanes hooker Andrew Hore decided to end a 2005 fishing trip with a couple of mates by taking some pot shots at a bunch of endangered fur seals, killing one. While Marine Mammal Sharpshooting is not an official Olympic sport, Hore definitely made a great case for its inclusion at a future event.

WHY IT'S SHIT: While in recent years the All Blacks have embraced cross-code superstars such as Brad Thorn and Sonny Bill Williams, Hore's attempt to defect to Marine Mammal Sharpshooting failed to capture the imagination of the sporting public and he was roundly condemned. Hore later retired from international rugby, in 2013.

Captain Hurricane

TOP 10 WORST NZ SPORTS MASCOTS

It's hard to define what makes a good sports mascot, but it's not hard to spot a terrible one. New Zealand definitely punches above its weight in terms of terrible sports mascots.

1. **CAPTAIN HURRICANE** (Rugby Union, Hurricanes)—Sporting a classic paedo moustache and flying a little plane called the 'Hurriplane' that doesn't actually fly, Captain Hurricane looks like your uncle who isn't invited to Christmas dinner anymore. Given the size of his pupils, the only way Captain Hurricane is getting high is by ingesting industrial quantities of cocaine. Bears an uncanny resemblance to the Harbourmaster, suggesting that there might be an *Avengers*-style team-up of molesty mascots in the offing.

2. **THE HARBOURMASTER** (Rugby Union, North Harbour)—A cartoon sea captain whose defining feature is a cleft chin that resembles a massive pair of hairless testicles. Presumably appeals to children's love of nautical-themed middle managers and scrotums.

3. **CAPTAIN BLUEBEARD** (Rugby Union, the Blues)—Continuing the City of Sails' love affair with dodgy nautical mascots is the Blues' cartoon pirate 'Captain Bluebeard'. Looking less like an actual pirate and more like a Ponsonby Road barista, Captain Bluebeard actually sported a blue goatee rather than a beard, adding false advertising to his vast array of crimes which almost certainly includes buggery on the high seas.

4. **STEELY DAN** (Rugby Union, Counties Manukau)—Like a shit knock-off of *X-Men*'s Colossus, Steely Dan is a man composed entirely of living steel. Steely Dan basically exists so drunk punters on the hill have an excuse to yell 'Hey Steely Dan, show us your steel balls!', a demand made more awkward by the fact that the mascot suit is probably worn by a fifteen-year-old female gymnast.

5. **BARRIE THE BUTCHER** (Rugby Union, Wanganui)—Looking like the identikit of someone who was seen running away from the Lundy residence, Barrie the Butcher features disorienting rhombus-shaped eyes and what can only be described as 'registered sex offender stubble'. He honours Whanganui's long history of brutal murder with a bloody cleaver and a gore-stained apron.

Steely Dan

Barrie the Butcher

6. **BDSM WARRIORS MASCOTS** (Rugby League, New Zealand Warriors)—A male and female couple clad in BDSM outfits who look like they've wandered onto the field after a long shift at a K Road dungeon. No rationale was supplied for adopting a pair of low-rent dominatrixes as the team's mascots, aside from possibly reflecting their fanbase's masochism and predilection for self-flagellation.

7. **TIKI** (Rugby League, New Zealand Warriors)—A truly low-effort attempt that is just someone in a Warriors uniform wearing the Warriors logo as a mask. Possibly arranged last minute after the Warriors spent all their design budget on their seventeenth alternate jersey for the upcoming season. The lack of imagination that has gone into Tiki is a true testament to the imagination and innovation that has gone into the Warriors' long commitment to mediocrity.

8. **HORI BOP** (Rugby Union, Bay of Plenty)—A morbidly obese man in a Bay of Plenty rugby jersey, Hori represents Bay of Plenty's commitment to gastronomic overindulgence and type-2 diabetes.

9. **MONZEE** (Netball, Waikato Bay of Plenty Magic)—Apparently designed to depict a young girl, Monzee is actually a grown woman wearing an oversized cartoon child's head. Resembling a paedophile's wet dream and

possibly a repurposed prop from some kind of Japanese porno, Monzee is a terrible idea for a mascot—the last thing that children are impressed by is another child. At least it gives the perverts something else to jack off to aside from the goal defence.

10. **GARY THE GLASS BARBIE** (Rugby League, Whangārei Flames)— Gary is an anthropomorphic methamphetamine pipe designed to celebrate Northland's love of the see-through didgeridoo. He also serves the vital purpose of educating children on how to deal with Dad if he's been up three days in a row and has decided to swap all the doors in the house for another point bag.

35: Rugby World Cup: turgid in Tokyo

WHAT HAPPENED: A heavily favoured All Blacks team gunning for their third consecutive World Cup title in 2019 instead came unstuck in their semi-final against a physically dominant England side prepared by All Blacks serial irritant Eddie Jones. If it hadn't been for winning the previous two Rugby World Cups, the whole country would have been plunged into its traditional six months of depression following an All Blacks World Cup loss.

WHY IT'S SHIT: Losing to the arrogant English is never an enjoyable experience, and this was only made worse by the fact it was masterminded by an Australian. The only silver lining to the loss was the fact that the arrogant Jones and his smug charges were summarily pummelled in the final by a rampant Springboks team. Perhaps the most shit aspect of the loss was the rather demure fashion in which the New Zealand sporting public accepted the All Blacks losing at the World Cup. Maybe it was due to the recent run of success, or perhaps New Zealand's waning reliance on the All Blacks as a source of national self-esteem. Still, such a limp effort was a pretty desultory conclusion to the glittering careers of All Blacks captain Kieran Read and coach Steve Hansen.[1]

---

1 Hansen, well known for usually displaying the emotional range of a burnt scone, verged on showing actual human emotion after the loss.

34: Silver Ferns' Comm Games flop

'We've come here to win a gold medal. To not win a medal, it's really, really hard.'—Katrina Grant, Silver Ferns captain

WHAT HAPPENED: Traditionally, netball has been played seriously by only two nations—Australia and New Zealand—and played well by one—Australia. New Zealand was comfortable with the fact that even though they were routinely thrashed by the Ockers, we were still better than the other countries who may or may not realise netball is an actual sport. Until the 2018 Gold Coast Commonwealth Games, that is. In pool play the Silver Ferns lost to Malawi, previously best known for being that place where Madonna nicks her kids from. They followed this impressive defeat by losing to England, which consigned them to a semi-final match-up with Jamaica, which they promptly lost.

WHY IT'S SHIT: Coming home empty-handed from the Commonwealth Games when a silver medal would have been considered mildly disappointing is fairly shit. Managing to lose to two teams who had never previously beaten the Silver Ferns was the second layer on a double-decker shit sandwich.

33: Dyer the liar

**'Dyer has to live with his conscience for the rest of his life—no way can I blame the umpires.'
—Alby Duckmanton, New Zealand team manager**

WHAT HAPPENED: Australian wicketkeeper Greg Dyer claimed a catch to dismiss Andrew Jones off the bowling of Craig McDermott during a test between Australia and New Zealand in Melbourne in 1987. However, the replays showed that he had clearly dropped the ball and regathered it.

WHY IT'S SHIT: While there's nothing surprising about an Australian cheating at cricket, the most shocking aspect of this incident was the sheer blatancy of the transgression—even the notoriously one-eyed Channel 9 commentary team called Dyer out. Amazingly, instead of conceding he'd made a mistake in the heat of battle, Dyer later doubled down and blamed the umpire! Unfortunately for Dyer, the existence of explicit video evidence and the fact that his surname rhymes with 'liar' meant he was never able to shake the implication that he had bullshitted to garner a dismissal, and his Australian cricket career ended shortly after when he was dropped in favour of a then-untested Ian Healy.

32: Rodney Redmond the one-test wonder

'At least I got the chance, albeit only once.'
—Rodney Redmond, NZ test cricketer

WHAT HAPPENED: Otago opener Rodney Redmond made his debut in the third test against Pakistan in 1973, as opening partner for Glenn Turner. Redmond marked the occasion by scoring a century in the first innings and a half-century in the second, a feat that wouldn't be matched by a New Zealand opener for another 40 years.

WHY IT'S SHIT: Despite the fact that New Zealand hasn't exactly been overburdened with top-quality opening batsmen throughout its cricketing history,[1] Redmond never played another test for New Zealand. He was included in the squad to tour England, but the selectors plumped for Northern Districts' John Parker to partner Turner against the Poms. While there were some suggestions that Redmond struggled with near-sightedness, his exclusion was almost certainly down to the fickle whims of the selectors. Poor old Rodney was left as a one-test wonder, destined to live on as the answer to a pub-quiz question. His son Aaron Redmond enjoyed a brief international career—slightly lengthier than his old man's but without a single ton to his name.

---

1   In fact, they could probably hold a reunion in a phone box and still have room for Jesse Ryder.

31: The umpire and the dominatrix

WHAT HAPPENED: In 1989, the New Zealand public was horrified when English cricket umpire Peter Plumley-Walker died during a bondage session at a Remuera flat, and teenage dominatrix Renée Chignell and her partner Neville Walker decided to dispose of the body by biffing it over the aptly named Huka Falls. Chignell and Walker were tried for murder three times but ultimately acquitted.

WHY IT'S SHIT: It's a well-known fact that all cricket umpires are sexual perverts—Frank Chester was a pissplay aficionado, David Shepherd loved a bit of pegging, and Shakoor Rana was a dab hand at autoerotic asphyxiation. Still, nobody in 1980s New Zealand was prepared for an umpire's private proclivities to be dragged out into the light in such a horrific fashion.

This case also broke New Zealand's BDSM cherry—prior to Plumley-Walker's untimely demise, 'bondage and discipline' sounded like a horse that finished fourth in the 1973 Melbourne Cup. Nobody should have been surprised—that moustache should have been a dead giveaway.

Chignell later opened a cricket-themed dungeon called 'The Corridor of Uncertainty'. The late umpire's contribution to the game has now been immortalised in a piece of cricketing slang—a strangle down the leg side is known as a 'Plumley-Walker'.

Alongside a ball counter and a light meter, handcuffs are an underrated part of the umpire's toolkit.

30: Australia steals Phar Lap

'The only way they're going to beat Phar Lap is if they breed a horse with wings and get Kingsford Smith to ride him.'—Jim Pike, jockey

WHAT HAPPENED: Kiwi-born thoroughbred Phar Lap was a legendary racehorse who won the hearts of two nations during the Depression. Known as the 'Wonder Horse' or 'Red Terror', the Timaru-born gelding won a Melbourne Cup, two Cox Plates, a Derby and nineteen other weight-for-age races, being declared an Australian hero in the process. He later died in mysterious circumstances ahead of a race in California.

WHY IT'S SHIT: For New Zealand's first genuine sporting star, getting 'Crowded Housed' before he could even race in his homeland and then murdered by some Yanks was a pretty ignominious foray onto the global sporting stage. Like pavlova, the flat white and problem drinking, Australia has a concerning habit of nicking some of New Zealand's best stuff and, like an equine Russell Crowe, Phar Lap was no exception. The horse's heritage was quickly dismissed as he was enthusiastically claimed by the Australian public. He appeared on Australian stamps, and one Perth local even suggested he be appointed Prime Minister.

As if being turned into an Aussie folk hero weren't bad enough, after Phar Lap's untimely death he suffered the further indignity of having his corpse divvied up like a KFC bucket—his hide residing in Melbourne, his skeleton in Wellington's Te Papa and his heart in the National Museum in Canberra. Despite his grisly fate, Phar Lap is still beloved in both countries, destined to haunt your nan's placemats forever.

29: Jack Bauer denied at the death

'I thought I had it, but then I realised in the last 50 metres that I had nothing.'—Jack Bauer, cyclist

WHAT HAPPENED: Early on in the fifteenth stage of the 2014 Tour de France, Garmin Sharp rider Jack Bauer opened up a commanding lead. The Kiwi put in the hard yards throughout the day to lead the pack for almost all of the 222-kilometre race—only to be passed by the charging peloton mere metres from the finish line, leaving him to cross in tenth place. In a moment, Bauer's childhood dream and a place in New Zealand sporting history vanished before his eyes.

WHY IT'S SHIT: In many ways, Bauer's cruel defeat encapsulates the stupidity of cycling as a sport. When a whole field of competitors can cower in an opponent's slipstream before snaking them at the death, the moral of the story is that hard work is a massive waste of time. Cycling is for two types of people: cowards, and middle-aged middle managers who drizzle themselves into crotch-squashing Lycra gimp suits to play chicken with traffic on Tamaki Drive before rewarding themselves with a bowl latte and a tug job in the bogs at Mission Bay. In fact, it's a stretch to even call it a sport when it's more a mere mode of transportation. Jack Bauer learnt his lesson the hard way when he tried to become New Zealand's first-ever Tour de France stage winner, but ended up being Sylvia Potts on a bike (see page 87).

28: Chiefs stampeded by Bulls

WHAT HAPPENED: The Chiefs reached their first Super Rugby[1] final in 2009 after defeating the Hurricanes 14–10 in the semi, setting up a showdown with the Bulls. Despite the long trek to Pretoria, hopes were high that the Mooloos could snare their first title. Unfortunately, the chaps from the Highveld had other ideas, determined to maintain their unbeaten record at the impregnable Loftus Versfeld. Piloted around by New Zealand rugby's favourite scapegoat Stephen Donald, the Chiefs managed to score first through Lelia Masaga but were quickly blown away by the Bulls' response, conceding four tries in swift succession on their way to being annihilated by a margin of 61–17, setting the record for the biggest-ever loss in a Super Rugby final.

WHY IT'S SHIT: Hamilton hadn't been so heartbroken since finding out that Woodstock didn't cure herpes. Coach Ian Foster later parlayed eight years of mediocrity at the helm of the Chiefs into a gig as All Blacks head coach, in a stunning example of failing upwards. The Chiefs would later win back-to-back titles under Dave Rennie, while Stephen Donald would go down in history as New Zealand's most famous whitebaiter.

---

1   At the time it was the Super 14 which came after the Super 12 which was before Super Rugby which was actually the Super 15 that became the Super 18 before going back to the Super 15.

NZ'S WORST SPORTING CLICHES

1. **'GAME OF TWO HALVES'**—No shit.

2. **'RUGBY WAS THE WINNER ON THE DAY'**—As opposed to the other sports which weren't actually played.

3. **'FULL CREDIT TO THE BOYS'**—Particularly awkward when used by a female athlete.

4. **'BACK OF THE OLD ONION BAG'**—This overused football phrase more readily brings to mind a scrotum than a goal.

5. **'HE'S TRAINING THE HOUSE DOWN!'**—It's unclear what the house did to deserve such treatment.

6. **'ONE-PERCENTERS'**—Less a critique of wealth disparity and more an indication of the average rugby player's mathematical proficiency.

7. **'TAKING IT ONE GAME AT A TIME'**—Rugby players seem to be able to experience time through a different simulacrum to everyone else.

8. **'SCOREBOARD PRESSURE'**—Seldom refers to the actual pressure of being crushed by a scoreboard.

27: Hungry, hungry halfbacks

WHAT HAPPENED: In 1954, the Wairarapa Bush provincial team were flying back to Masterton after losing a bitter contest to hated rivals Poverty Bay, when their Douglas DC-6 got lost in fog over the Ureweras and crashed into the side of a mountain. Fearful that they would not be found and desperate for a post-match feed, the team quickly turned to cannibalism. Fortunately, none of the players had perished in the crash. Unfortunately for Arnie Trow, the halfback drew the short straw and sacrificed one of his rather meaty thighs to satiate the team's lust for human flesh.

WHY IT'S SHIT: Sadly, Arnie's sacrifice was largely in vain as it transpired that the plane had gone down only 200 metres off State Highway 2. The team had been missing for about 45 minutes when they resorted to their act of premature cannibalism. In the years that followed, Trow recounted his ordeal with good humour, and with the aid of a solid kauri prosthetic he later recovered enough to travel with the All Blacks on their 1957 tour of Finland, playing a couple of midweek matches.

The legacy of the horrific incident still lingers today, with opposing fans still referring to the team as the 'Bloody Bush'. The whole gory episode served as the inspiration for the 1993 film *Alive* starring Sam Neill as Darb Tarplin and Michael Hurst as Arnie Trow.

The DC-10 was no match for the bulk of a fully tanked up forward pack following a post-match function.

26: Rugby World Cup: full Gregan

'Four more years!'—George Gregan, Wallabies scrum half

WHAT HAPPENED: 2003: Another Rugby World Cup, another All Blacks team losing in disappointing fashion. Led by a combination of John Mitchell, the most reviled All Blacks coach in recent memory, and Reuben Thorne, the most invisible All Blacks captain in recent memory, this particular All Blacks team were strong favourites to hoist the trophy. Having trounced the Wallabies earlier in the year by 50, the ABs were confident they could get over their rivals in the semi-final.

Foiled by a ferocious Wallabies defence and struggling to impose themselves physically, the All Blacks failed to make a mark. Australia finished out winners 22–10. It wouldn't be the last time Eddie Jones thwarted the All Blacks' Rugby World Cup ambitions, but it might be the most annoying.

WHY IT'S SHIT: Famous for Gregan's now iconic sledge, a masterpiece of both economy and cruelty, this match is underrated in terms of All Blacks suffering. As hard as it is to fathom now, this was an era when the Wallabies regularly beat the All Blacks, and each loss was salted with that stomach-turning sight of a victorious Australian.

The decision to play fullback Leon MacDonald out of position at centre is one of the dumbest selection decisions made by the All Blacks for a crucial match. It's one thing to lose a match to Gallic volatility (see World Cup 1999 or 2007) or a duplicitous waitress (see World Cup 1995), but to lose due to a series of selection blunders is especially galling.

The loss continued the long national nightmare that began in 1991 and had seen the All Blacks fall short in four consecutive Rugby World Cups. For a country that assumed the World Cup was invented for them to win, this prolonged period of futility caused serious damage to the national self-esteem—it got so bad that New Zealanders started caring about yachting!

Following the loss, John Mitchell was sacked and replaced by Graham Henry who (eventually) brought home another World Cup title, so it worked out in the end.

25: Warriors lose first grand final

'I got caught up in the moment—just looking around thinking "wow, this is awesome". Then, before you knew it, the game was over.'—Clinton Toopi, Warriors centre

WHAT HAPPENED: In 2002, two years after going bust, the New Zealand Warriors unexpectedly snaffled the minor premiership after the Bulldogs were stripped of their points for repeated salary-cap breaches. Led by 'the Little General' Stacey Jones, and featuring a cast of characters including the flinty Kevin Campion and fan favourite Mark Tookey, the Warriors employed an exhilarating ad-lib brand of footy that excited their fans and actually won some games. After securing the minor premiership, the Warriors defeated the Canberra Raiders and the Cronulla Sharks to book a place in the grand final against a star-studded Sydney Roosters side, featuring all-time great Brad Fittler and a host of Origin stars.

Prior to the season kick-off, few Warriors fans thought their team had the ability to challenge for a title, but now they dared to dream. In a bad pre-match omen, rock star Billy Idol was due to perform but had to abandon the gig due to a power outage. Despite a promising start to the match and keeping the game close into the final quarter, the Warriors were eventually no match for the Roosters' star power. Sydney ended up winning 30–8.

WHY IT'S SHIT: For Warriors fans to stand on the precipice of ultimate glory so soon after facing financial obliteration was almost unthinkable. Despite losing their maiden grand-final appearance, the future suddenly looked bright for the previously rudderless Warriors. Hard-nosed Australian coach Daniel Anderson had welded a contingent of mercurial Aussie veterans into a homegrown core of burgeoning superstars. Players like Ali Lauiti'iti, Henry Fa'afili and Lance Hohaia were on the verge of becoming household names. Anything seemed possible. Unfortunately 'anything' also includes 'complete and total collapse'. While they made the finals the following season, the Warriors fell short of the decider within two seasons from their first grand final appearance. Anderson had been sacked, Jones was plying his trade in the south of France and the Warriors had recorded their worst season ever. The club would not reach the grand final again until 2011 which they also managed to lose. The Warriors have now gone over 25 years with no silverware to show for it.

24: Carlaw catastrophe: Kiwis lose to South Africa

WHAT HAPPENED: Following a 1963 Australian tour in which the South African league team lost to everyone they played (including the Parramatta Eels), they arrived for the New Zealand leg of their tour.

The tourists were so depleted by injuries that two Australian club players were drafted in just so they could field a full starting line-up. In the lead-up to the match, South Africa managed to lose to the South Island and an Auckland side that was a virtual B-team due to the majority of their players being in camp with the Kiwis. It was a miserable bludger of a game played in the Carlaw Park slop, the overwhelming stench of piss wafting up from the overflowing bogs in the Railway Stand. South Africa finished out victors 4–3.

WHY IT'S SHIT: South Africa is not renowned as one of the great rugby league nations. In fact, they generally occupy a spot in the world rankings somewhere between Vanuatu and Bulgaria. If you asked your average Warriors fan, they would be pretty surprised to find out that the braai boys have been fielding rugby league teams of varying degrees of suckitude for decades. To date, this is the only meeting between the two nations, meaning South Africa can claim a 100 per cent winning record. Don't expect a rematch anytime soon.

23: New Zealand hill-climbing team thrashed on Turkish tour

WHAT HAPPENED: The combined New Zealand and Australian Competitive Hill Climbing team travelled to Gallipoli in 1915 with high hopes. This was the Australasian Hill Climbing team's first international tour and a large squad was selected, numbering in the thousands. Unfortunately, they copped a rough draw and ended up facing the very formidable Turkish team on home soil. Powered by Anzac biscuits and an unquestioned belief in God, King and Country, the New Zealanders gave it their best shot but ultimately ended up suffering a grievous loss.

WHY IT'S SHIT: The competitive hill-climbing scene in New Zealand never really recovered from the thorough thrashing the Kiwi contingent received at Gallipoli. Indeed, even now 'Gallipoli' is a byword for a sound hiding—for example, 'the Warriors are Gallipolli'd on a regular basis'. Much like the All Blacks' loss to France in Cardiff, New Zealand now marks the loss at Gallipoli with an annual ceremony.

22: Spinning Rhombus forgets to jump

'By the time he'd hit six, I was wishing I was somewhere else.'—Andrew Nicholson, equestrian rider

WHAT HAPPENED: Following the dressage and steeplechase events at the 1992 Barcelona Olympics, Andrew Nicholson and his mount Spinning Rhombus were odds-on favourites to bag a gold medal. On show-jumping day, Spinning Rhombus (or 'Piggy', as he was known) had a meltdown.[1] He hit the third obstacle hard and spent the rest of his round refusing to jump. Like a four-legged Jean van de Velde, Piggy continued to choke. At six rails it seemed like something of an elaborate prank. All told, Spinning Rhombus knocked down nine rails and Nicholson did well to convince the errant steed to complete the course and hang onto silver.

WHY IT'S SHIT: New Zealand on the whole has an uneasy relationship with equestrian—it seems a bit poncy and probably isn't really a sport, but then on the other hand we sometimes win Olympic medals.[2] It involves something called 'dressage', which sounds suspiciously like making costumes for horses. In fact, the only bit of equestrian that

---

1   In fact, it was fair to say he had a right 'mare.

2   It's safe to say that if cooking meth or performing your own dental work were Olympic sports and New Zealand had a medal hope, the whole country would be behind them.

most Kiwis understand is show jumping—it's like steeplechase for horses that went to private school. Suffice to say, Spinning Rhombus' efforts in Barcelona didn't inspire a generation of schoolchildren to take up equestrian.

21: Inzamam-ul-Haq goes batshit

WHAT HAPPENED: Largely unfancied leading into the 1992 Cricket World Cup, a plucky and innovative New Zealand team went on an unprecedented run through pool play based on a slew of revolutionary tactics. The previously languid Mark Greatbatch was reinvented as an explosive opener who took the attack to the bowlers in a fashion hitherto unseen in the short form. Off-spinner Dipak Patel opened the bowling. An armada of 'dibbly dobblies' choked opposing batsmen on stodgy New Zealand wickets. The use of aggressive fielding marked the first time the discipline had been seen as a match-winning skill.

The tournament also provided some iconic images in the history of New Zealand cricket: Chris Harris running out David Boon with only one stump to aim at. Martin Crowe scampering through to bring up his ton against Australia. Everything was falling New Zealand's way—until the quarter-final.

New Zealand's only loss in the round robin was to Pakistan in Christchurch. Conversely, their opponents had overcome a poor start to the competition and snuck into the semi after flogging Australia in their final round-robin game. Inspirational skipper Martin Crowe pulled his hamstring, but New Zealand still managed to amass a then-imposing 262. Pakistan were 140/4 after 35 overs, a seemingly insurmountable lead in the pre-T20 era of cricket. It was then that Sayed Inzamam-ul-Haq, a relatively unknown 22-year-old with the turning speed of an oil tanker and the caloric intake of a diabetic camel, strode to the wicket. Inzamam-ul-Haq detonated on the Kiwi bowling attack, smashing a then-unprecedented 60 off only 37 balls. Without Crowe on the field to marshal his bowlers, it seemed like the spell that the flotilla of medium-pacers had woven on opposing batsmen was broken. Inzamam-ul-Haq was ultimately run out by a direct hit by Harris, but it was too little, too late—Pakistan needed only another 36 runs, and for New Zealand the game was lost.

WHY IT'S SHIT: New Zealand had entered the competition with no great expectations of success, but the manner of their elimination seemed particularly cruel. With their inspirational skipper sidelined, the nation watched the young underdogs they had thrown themselves behind crumple beneath the onslaught of the unheralded Inzamam-ul-Haq. This would be New Zealand's first devastating exit from the final stages of a World Cup, but it would hardly be their last.

TOP 10
RUGBY PARKS

1. Rugby Park, Invercargill

2. Rugby Park, Hamilton

3. Rugby Park, Greymouth

4. Rugby Park, New Plymouth

5. Rugby Park, Whakatāne

6. Rugby Park, Gisborne

7. Rugby Park, Huntly

8. Rugby Park, Whangārei

9. Rugby Park, Christchurch

10. Rugby Park, Te Kuiti

20: Rugby World Cup: sacré blergh!

WHAT HAPPENED: The All Blacks strode into the 1999 Rugby World Cup—the first of the professional era—as firm favourites to lift the Webb Ellis for the second time. Unfortunately, fate and some dastardly Frenchmen had other plans.

After topping Scotland 30–18 in the quarter-final, the All Blacks faced a French side that had slipped past Argentina in their quarter-final match-up. The heavily favoured All Blacks started strong, leading 24–10 early in the second stanza thanks to a brace of tries by the iconic Jonah Lomu. Then the unthinkable happened: France scored 33 unanswered points to snatch victory from the jaws of defeat and leave the All Blacks befuddled losers.

WHY IT'S SHIT: This was the beginning of the long national nightmare. The loss to England in 1991 had featured an ageing All Blacks team that needed to be refreshed, and while the manner of 1995's loss was heartbreaking, it was hard to argue with the idea that New Zealand had just run into the jaws of history.[1]

The All Blacks went on to lose the third-place play-off (AKA 'the over-pants handie' game).

---

1   While the manner of 1995's grand final defeat to South Africa was heartbreaking, the only people who don't love a smiling Nelson Mandela are the most ardent All Blacks fans and two-thirds of the population of Browns Bay.

19: NZ Knights kicked out of A-League

WHAT HAPPENED: The Knightmare began with the Auckland-based Football Kingz in 1999, a club that was a catalogue of catastrophes. Alarm bells started ringing when the country's first professional football team adopted a truly humiliating moniker, combining a deliberate misspelling with a culturally irrelevant mascot, and apparently being too embarrassed to include Auckland in their name. 'Football Kingz' sounded more like a shit street gang than a sports team. After two middling seasons in Australia's National Soccer League under player-coach Wynton Rufer, the Kingz sacked the living legend as coach, to which he responded by retiring as a player. What followed were three consecutive finishes in the bottom three, including two wooden spoons, with crowd numbers barely breaking 1000, before the club disbanded in disgrace.

Just when things couldn't get any worse, they did. The Kingz were restructured into the New Zealand Knights—a brand much less embarrassing but just as meaningless—who entered the A-League for its inaugural season. The Knights were soon revealed to be as out of their depth in the new Australian competition as the Kingz were in the old one, finishing dead last in two seasons before being unceremoniously booted out of the league for their poor performances and low attendances. They were replaced in the A-League by the Wellington Phoenix, bringing an end to Auckland's disastrous experiment in professional football.

WHY IT'S SHIT: The Kingz/Knights debacle not only put Auckland football fans through seven years of torment, but potentially cost the city any chance of hosting a professional football team again. Impressive crowd numbers at the Phoenix's Auckland games prove that Aucklanders will turn up to watch a team if it's not being hopelessly mismanaged—yet the Kingz and the Knights will be forefront in the minds of decision-makers if the A-League ever receives another application from the Super City. It speaks volumes about their predecessors that a team as consistently mediocre as the Wellington Phoenix (AKA the Warriors of football) is seen as a success. Football fans will tolerate their players pretending to cry to win free kicks, rooting each other's wives and karate-kicking the odd fan, but even they have a limit.

18: Kiwi traitors win America's Cup for Alinghi

'This must rank as one of the most traitorous moves in New Zealand sporting history.'—*The Evening Post*

WHAT HAPPENED: In 2003, America's Cup holders Team New Zealand were challenged for the trophy by Alinghi, funded by pharmaceutical magnate Ernesto Bertarelli. Controversially, the Swiss syndicate was headed by former Team New Zealand skipper Russell Coutts and tactician Brad Butterworth, New Zealand's second-most-hated pirates (after the blokes who murdered Peter Blake). Following the defection of Coutts and Butterworth, the New Zealand sporting public had been shocked to discover that giant piles of money had outranked national pride, and quickly turned on the pair. Team New Zealand responded by naming human polo-shirt Dean Barker skipper and enlisting Dave Dobbyn to belt out 'Loyal' as a theme song. Unfortunately, the groundswell of public support and a banging theme tune failed to stack up against Alinghi's superior boat and better crew, and the 'Swiss' defeated Team New Zealand 5–0 to claim the Auld Mug.

WHY IT'S SHIT: After getting over the ignominy of losing a yacht race to a country with no coastline, which is a bit like losing a swimming race to a country without a pool, the fact that the victory was masterminded by a pair of Kiwi-heroes-turned-mercenaries simply rubbed salt into the wound.

Treachery aside, the most shit thing about Alinghi's victory was that it shone a light on the lie at the heart of the America's Cup: instead of being a competition between plucky sailing nations deploying skill and innovation in a clash upon the waves, it was pretty much just Formula One for guys in Lacoste polos. Billionaires unfortunately have little regard for red socks and our crippling national lack of self-esteem.

17: The Gregan tackle

'It will follow me around for the rest of my life.'—Jeff Wilson, former All Black

WHAT HAPPENED: A one-off 1994 Bledisloe test in Sydney was going down to the wire. The All Blacks had valiantly battled back to within one score after entering the second half down 17–6. With moments left, dual-sport wunderkind Jeff Wilson beat several defenders before stepping past Damian Smith to dart for the corner for what would be the winning try. Wallabies halfback George Gregan appeared out of nowhere to ensnare Wilson in a desperate, last-ditch tackle, knocking the ball loose as Wilson dived to score. The Wallabies escaped with a 20–16 victory.

WHY IT'S SHIT: It's hard to envisage a more iconic image of Kiwi sporting futility: Jeff Wilson, a golden hero, being stripped of the ball mere inches from the tryline, the match literally slipping through his fingers as Gregan raked the ball loose.

Today, the infamous tackle provides a sort of odd nostalgia for a time when the All Blacks actually needed valiant comebacks to vanquish the Wallabies. Given that the Aussies haven't posed a serious challenge to New Zealand's Bledisloe dominance in about 30 years, it serves as an almost quaint reminder of when the Wallabies were an actual rugby team.

16: Buck busts a nut

'They each had their little pill in front of their plates for the meal before the match. The All Blacks realised that their opponents, unrecognisable from the previous week, were loaded.'—Jacques Mombet, French team doctor

WHAT HAPPENED: Between nuclear testing and terrorist attacks the French were certainly intent on becoming New Zealand's nemesis during the 1980s. However it was an incident on the rugby pitch that might have proven the most egregious. The All Blacks toured France in 1986 for a two-match series, winning the first test in Toulouse 19–7. The second match would go down in history as the 'Battle of Nantes', an ill-tempered affair that was less a rugby match and more of a bar brawl crossed with a prison riot played out over 80 minutes. For reasons that will become clear the match would also catapult Buck Shelford into the pantheon of All Black heroes. In a bid to reverse the result of the first test, the French team were allegedly hopped up on more amphetamines than Antonie Roni Dixon on payday, and attacked the game with the sort of ferocity they usually reserved for a wheel of brie or having an extramarital affair. The All Blacks were on the receiving end of an absolute savaging as the French dished out the sort of brutality seldom seen in the modern game. At one point Shelford's scrotum was torn open, exposing his Bucksticle. For most mere mortals, this would be enough to send them screaming from the field. Shelford merely asked the physio to stitch up his ballsack and returned to the fray, refusing to leave the game. He eventually came off the field but not until he was knocked unconscious in the second half, losing several teeth in the process.

WHY IT'S SHIT: The incident was the biggest crime against male genitalia until Lorena Bobbitt picked up a carving knife. The French would go onto become the All Blacks bogey and the savagery of this match would be cited nearly as frequently as their Gallic flair. Shelford's heroics in the match set an impossibly high bar for the standard of Kiwi manliness—unless you'd had your scrotum torn open by a rusty sprig and finished a game of rugby then you were basically half a poof. On the plus side, coach Brian Lochore cited the vicious loss as the catalyst for the All Blacks' victory at the 1987 Rugby World Cup, so at least Buck didn't suffer in vain.

15: Sylvia Potts' infamous trip

WHAT HAPPENED: Two metres from the finish line in the 1500 metres final at the 1970 Edinburgh Commonwealth Games, race leader Sylvia Potts tripped over. She eventually recovered to finish ninth. Potts' dive would go down as the most famous fall in New Zealand history until Cave Creek.

WHY IT'S SHIT: It's hard to imagine a more iconic image of a shit sports moment—mere steps from victory, Potts lies sprawled on the track, helplessly watching her competitors steam past her to glory. She was lucky that her tumble happened in the pre-internet era—nowadays such an iconic fail would have resulted in meme immortality. While the incident was a perfect example of the sheer agony of sport, in true Kiwi fashion Potts picked herself up because she had another race the next day. Potts would go on to have a long and storied career coaching athletics with her husband Allan, serving as New Zealand athletics team manager at the 1990 Commonwealth Games. Her trip later gained international attention thanks to the 2004 Snoop Dogg single 'Drop it Like it's Potts'.

14: Ref ruins Original All Blacks tour

'It was a try, you know.'—Bob Deans' last words

WHAT HAPPENED: The All Blacks' first tour of the Northern Hemisphere in 1905 would set the standard for all tours that would follow, with 27 wins from 28 games played. The Originals' only loss was to Wales, a defeat steeped in controversy. Played in front of a crowd of 47,000 at Cardiff Arms Park, the game ended dramatically after Scottish referee John Dallas, 30 metres behind the play, ruled that halfback Bob Deans had failed to ground the ball while reaching out to score the game-winning try. The dubious decision resulted in the solitary defeat of the Originals' tour, 3–0.

WHY IT'S SHIT: All Black Dave Gallaher later accepted the defeat with the resolute good grace that would set the template for all future All Blacks skippers. Given that it was decades before the advent of talkback radio or social media, it's unclear how disappointed All Blacks fans were across the nation—although it is safe to assume copious amounts of liquor and domestic violence were involved. Like an Edwardian Wayne Barnes, Dallas would exist as the pre-eminent referee scapegoat until Barnes himself took the title 102 years later.

13: Black Caps hit an all-time low

'We weren't professionals you see. There was no such thing as a professional in those days.'—J.R. Reid, New Zealand captain

WHAT HAPPENED: In 1955, after posting a competitive 200 in the first innings and holding the vaunted English tourists to a paltry 46-run lead, hopes were high that New Zealand could press for their first victory in cricket over the mother country. Instead, New Zealand capitulated for an almost absurd 26, a figure that still stands as the lowest ever total in test cricket. It would be another 23 years before New Zealand recorded their first test victory over England.

WHY IT'S SHIT: Described as 'the darkest day in New Zealand cricket', this is one hyperbolic claim that might actually ring true. Batting on an uncovered pitch against a team of professionals, New Zealand set an almost impossibly low total that will never be surpassed in the record books.

Great cricketing nations such as Zimbabwe, Bangladesh and Ireland have all since made their test debuts and never come remotely close to threatening New Zealand's all-time low. Given the quality of coaching, equipment and preparation today, it seems almost unthinkable that New Zealand will ever lose this record—unless the Karachi bookmakers have something to say about it.

TOP 10 WORST HAIRCUTS IN NZ SPORT

1. **JONAH LOMU** (Rugby Union)— He may have been a rugby legend, but Lomu's iconic hair tuft gave the impression he'd had his hair cut by the council.

2. **JASON EATON** (Rugby Union)— Massive mullets, elaborate moustaches and caveman beards—former All Black and Hurricane Jason Eaton's commitment to a crook lid is legendary.

3. **JUSTIN MARSHALL** (Rugby Union)—Marshall's frosted tips were the kind of haircut that gets you beaten up in a Queenstown strip club. Boomfa!

4. **JACK GOODHUE** (Rugby Union)— Current mantle-holder of the worst hair in world rugby, All Black Jack Goodhue probably would have been taken behind the clubrooms and administered a thorough beating in days gone by for his truly sickening mullet.

5. **DAVID TUA** (Boxing)—Tua's early 2000s effort made him look like he'd just made love to an electric fence.

6. **TAWERA NIKAU** (Rugby League)—Former NRL and Kiwis lock Tawera Nikau didn't have a leg to stand on when it came to his horrendous flowing mullet.

7. **HAMISH MARSHALL** (Cricket)—Marshall's trademark curls were converted into the world's worst white-guy afro for a T20 clash against Australia.

8. **HEATH DAVIS** (Cricket)—New Zealand's answer to Dennis Rodman, Davis obviously spent more time at the hairdresser than working on his chronic no-ball problem.

9. **CARL BULFIN** (Cricket)—The Central District's paceman may have been the only person in the history of first-class cricket to saunter to the wicket in peroxide dreadlocks and Dirty Dog sunnies. While an iconic look for Rhythm and Vines, Bulfin's locks did not prove a hit on the pitch.

10. **JAKE ROBERTSON** (Athletics)—I'd run too if I had a mullet like that.

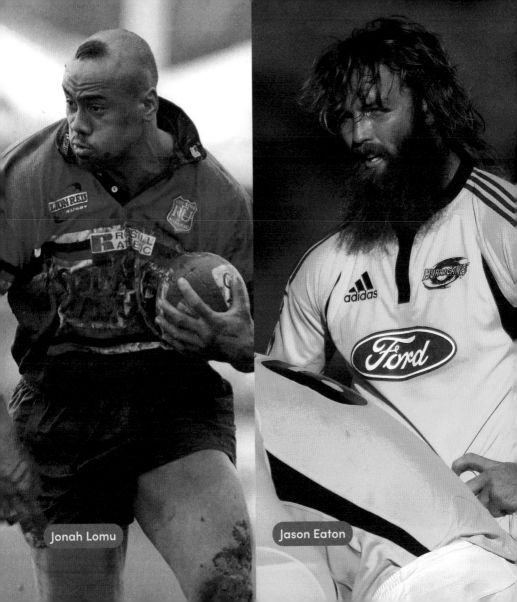

Jonah Lomu

Jason Eaton

12: Puff, puff, Paarl

'To think that NZC knew that there were others involved, who were far more senior and established than the three youngsters. It was pretty sick, really.'—Ken Rutherford, Black Caps captain

WHAT HAPPENED: In 1994, the first Kiwi test team to visit South Africa in 30 years started with a bang, recording a famous test-match victory in Johannesburg by 137 runs—New Zealand's first victory in the republic since the series of 1961/62. After getting wrecked in a One Day Quad Series involving the hosts, Sri Lanka and Pakistan, New Zealand faced a Boland XI ahead of the second test. Following the match, some of their opponents broke out a spliff, and a handful of Black Caps partook in their hosts' hospitality. This minor indiscretion later turned into a storm in a bong bowl after an anonymous snitch ratted out his teammates. The inter-squad tension boiled over onto the field, with New Zealand getting soundly thrashed in both subsequent matches. The Black Caps became the first team since 1888 to lose a three-match series after winning the first match.

Upon returning home, young squad members Dion Nash, Matthew Hart and Stephen Fleming were exposed to the sort of public trial usually reserved only for Dunedin paperboys, and received three-match bans. Chris Pringle would later admit his involvement and receive a ban for 'inadequately preparing for a test match', which is a fantastic euphemism for getting high.

WHY IT'S SHIT: Kiwis hate a grass (unless they happen to be rolling it into a fat joint). The identity of the nark has never been officially established, but several amateur sleuths believe they have fingered the offender. Meanwhile, the public were left with the distinct impression that Nash, Hart and Fleming had been hung out to dry by the administrators. As far as cricketing controversies go, passing around a reefer seems almost quaint compared to drink-driving,[1] ball tampering[2] or accusations of match-fixing.[3] Still, the stink of the whole affair lingered over New Zealand cricket for years to come. Skipper Ken Rutherford ended up losing the captaincy, and the remainder of the '90s were a bleak era in the history of the Black Caps. For a tour which started out so promisingly to be derailed by a single joint is pretty shit.

---

1 See Ryder, Jesse.
2 See Smith, Steve and Warner, David.
3 See Cronje, Hansie; Vincent, Lou; and Pakistan cricket team, all of.

11: NZ blank at Moscow Olympics

'It's a wound that won't heal. I don't think you ever do get over it.'—Brian Newth, New Zealand pentathlete

WHAT HAPPENED: In 1980, for the first and only time in its sporting history as a stand-alone country, New Zealand failed to win a single medal at an Olympic Games. That's correct—not a single medal! A total of 203 events were contested in Moscow, and New Zealand didn't register even one podium finish, easily our worst performance at an Olympics. Utter disgrace.

WHY IT'S SHIT: Do you know how bad you have to be to win zero medals at an Olympics? Terrible. Here's a list of some of the countries that didn't win a medal at the 2016 Rio de Janeiro Olympics: Kosovo, South Sudan and the Vatican City (two of which were recently involved in civil wars and one of which may actually be an elaborate means to avoid child molestation charges rather than being a sovereign nation). After our entirely abject performance at the 1980 Moscow Olympics, New Zealand was forced to take a good hard look at ourselves, and dedicated our efforts to the sort of sports that we excel at: mostly those dominated by other white countries and where you can sit down the whole time, such as rowing, yachting and cycling. If taking a shit is ever an Olympic event, then we're a shoo-in for gold.

10: Cake Tin calamity: Kiwis lose to Fiji

'The most disappointing thing for me is that everyone who doubted us—the fans, media—yous got your way.'—Shaun Johnson, Kiwis halfback

WHAT HAPPENED: For the most part Kiwis fans have simple expectations of any global competition—generally the Kiwis will roll through the group stage, putting minnows to the sword before facing England in a semi for the opportunity to get curb-stomped by the Kangaroos in the final, content in the knowledge that the Kangaroos play a bad game about once a decade. Losing to Mate Ma'a Tonga in the pool play at the 2017 Rugby League World Cup was an acceptable aberration—the game was a cracker and the emergence of Tonga as a genuine force was the most exciting thing to happen to the game in years. Even after the loss, the Kiwis were still a good shout to make the grand final and get embarrassed by the Kangaroos in predictable fashion. Instead, they managed to lose a tryless bludger of a quarter-final to rugby league minnow Fiji, 4–2. Fortunately, the players obviously understood the fans' disappointment and decided to double down by blaming the loss on everybody else including the fans, the media and the hot dog vendor. Astoundingly, captain Adam Blair described the unprecedented loss as 'not a negative' and claimed 'I'm proud of what we've created', presumably in the same way that toddlers are proud of taking a shit in a pot plant.

WHY IT'S SHIT: The Kiwis losing to Fiji would be like the All Blacks losing to Fiji. Losing to Fiji *without scoring a single try* seems vaguely inconceivable. For coach David Kidwell, losing a quarter-final to Fiji was possibly the most embarrassing thing a Kiwis coach could do (aside from coaching the Warriors).

For the fans, Shaun Johnson's churlish response betrayed the lie that sits at the heart of all organised sport: that the players probably don't care about the outcome of the game nearly as much as the people cheering from the sidelines.

Fortunately, most Kiwis fans are also Warriors fans so they are familiar with half-hearted performances and inexplicable losses. If the All Blacks were subject to such a quarter-final embarrassment there would almost certainly be massive consequences—like re-appointing Graham Henry as coach and blaming the whole thing on Wayne Barnes. Unfortunately there was no Wayne Barnes, Kidwell got the sack and the New Zealand sporting public went back to thinking of the Kiwis as the second most disappointing league team in the country after the Warriors.

9: All-white All Blacks

WHAT HAPPENED: The All Blacks toured South Africa in 1960, a trip that is now best remembered for the fact that no Māori players were selected due to South Africa's racist apartheid policies. More than 150,000 New Zealanders signed a petition opposing the tour, horrified by the prospect of assuaging racists by using a Dulux colour chart to pick the squad. The outrage prompted the protest slogan 'No Maoris, No Tour' and even a parody of '*My Old Man's a Dustman*' by one of the Howard Morrison Quartet. Despite widespread demonstrations, the tour went ahead.

WHY IT'S SHIT: For a little country that prides itself on punching above its weight when it comes to doing the right thing, the 1960 All Blacks tour of South Africa is a pretty big black mark on our record (pun definitely intended). All-white All Blacks squads had previously toured the apartheid state in 1928 and 1949, but by 1960 the mood of the nation was starting to swing away from such blatant racism. Fortunately, the Rugby Union managed to rectify the situation by ensuring that Māori players were able to tour in 1970 and 1976, albeit only with the disgusting designation 'honorary whites'. New Zealand's continued rugby association with apartheid South Africa would result in the entire African continent boycotting the 1976 Olympic Games in Montréal, before simmering tensions within New Zealand came to a head in 1981.

CITIZENS ALL BLACK TOUR ASSOCIATION

PROTEST MEETING

WELLINGTON TOWN HALL — WEDNESDAY 12th AUG. at 8 p.m.

NO MAORIS - NO TOUR

To fight racial discrimination in the selection of the 1960 All Black team to tour South Africa. This is an issue vital to every New Zealander. Racial discrimination must be fought right here in New Zealand.

Don't miss this meeting. Those coming in support from Hawke's Bay and North Auckland include:
GEORGE NEPIA and LOUIE PAEWAI
of the famous 1924 "Invincibles"
and VINCE BEVAN and M. N. PAEWAI.

ROLLAND O'REGAN, Chairman, C.A.B.T.A.

8: Silver Ferns choke away the World Cup

'I know it's not all my fault, but I still take responsibility for it.'—Donna Loffhagen, Silver Fern

WHAT HAPPENED: Leading old rivals Australia 34–28 at three-quarter-time in the 1999 Netball World Cup final, the Silver Ferns managed to pull off a choke job worthy of Linda Lovelace. Following a fierce Aussie comeback, Donna Loffhagen missed a close-range penalty shot to clinch the match with 20 seconds remaining. Sharelle McMahon then scored at the other end to give Australia the 42–41 win and their third world title in a row.

WHY IT'S SHIT: Much like a horror-movie villain, Australian sports teams are never dead and buried until the head is decapitated, the body burnt to a cinder and whatever remains is flung into the sun. In true Kiwi sports-fan fashion, young goal-shooter Loffhagen wore most of the blame for the capitulation, despite the fact that the rest of the team was equally responsible for coughing up an eight-point lead in the final quarter.

7: Valerie Adams and the drug cheat

'The worst thing about it for me was she took the moment [London] away. That's probably what hurts the most.'—Valerie Adams, Olympic shot-putter

WHAT HAPPENED: In the run-up to the London Olympics, Valerie Adams was the hot favourite to repeat her success in Beijing with another gold medal. Adams was one of New Zealand's most successful and popular Olympians, tapping into Aotearoa's previously unexplored love for large women throwing things long distances. From a Kiwi perspective, the 2012 Olympics were less a competition and more of a coronation for our Queen Val. Unfortunately, a devious Eastern European had something else in mind.

Despite looking like Chris Farley on a comedown, Nadzeya Ostapchuk nailed four throws of over 21 metres to claim gold. Clearly rattled by her opponent's sudden surge in ability and needing a personal best to claim gold, Adams failed to step up to the mark, breaking a streak of 24 consecutive wins and breaking hearts all across New Zealand. To our nation's shock, Adams had somehow been beaten by a Belarusian. Not even a proper Russian!

WHY IT'S SHIT: Most New Zealand sports fans would struggle to find Belarus on a map, and didn't know much about the former Soviet state aside from the fact that they sound like the bad guys in a Sylvester Stallone movie. Combined with the fact that Ostapchuk looked like she let her cellmate cut her hair, suspicions quickly arose about the legitimacy of her victory. Two weeks later, New Zealanders' least charitable suspicions were confirmed when Ostapchuk tested positive for anabolic steroids and was stripped of her medal, promoting Val to gold. It didn't matter. Adams was later awarded her medal in a ceremony at Auckland's Cloud event centre, a world away from the glory of an Olympic podium.

6: Rugby World Cup: forward pass my arse

'If we played that match again, five times out of six we would lose it.'—Bernard Laporte, France coach

WHAT HAPPENED: It's still hard to believe, but in 2007, New Zealand was knocked out of the Rugby World Cup at the lowly quarter-final stage. Weighed down by the expectations of a nation and a history of stumbling in big games (see World Cup 1995, World Cup 1999, World Cup 2003, etc), the All Blacks succumbed to a French side doing an inordinate number of French things. Of course, the New Zealand rugby public took the loss with its typical good grace and blamed it all on the referee.

In retrospect, the seeds of the All Blacks' loss were sown prior to kick-off. There were suggestions that they had been delivered a soft schedule in pool play, leaving them underprepared for the rigours of knockout rugby. Odd selections such as Luke McAlister ahead of Aaron Mauger, and Keith Robinson instead of Chris Jack, were made with an eye on what was seen as an inevitable semi-final berth.

The French approached the game with a smothering aggression, blanketing the All Blacks with savage defence and refusing to allow them into the game. The clinching try scored by Yannick Jauzion seemed to be set up by a blatant forward pass by centre David Marty, a clear breach overlooked by referee Wayne Barnes.

WHY IT'S SHIT: This was the All Blacks' worst-ever World Cup result, the first time they had failed to reach the last four. For New Zealand rugby fans, Cardiff would henceforth bear the sombre resonance of Gallipoli or the Alamo. The bitter nature of the loss took the continuing national neurosis about the All Blacks' inability to win another Rugby World Cup and turned it into a full-blown mania. Prior to this defeat, it was inconceivable that the All Blacks could be eliminated at such an early stage of the tournament. For an insecure rugby-obsessed nation, it prompted the sort of desperate soul-searching normally reserved for accidentally wanking off over a bloke—what went wrong? Was this something to do with the *Rainbow Warrior*? Did we have to join Australia now?

Based on the referee's controversial call and the fact that the All Blacks were awarded only two penalties in the entire match, Barnes formed a convenient scapegoat for a wounded nation and was convicted largely on the fact he was English. He later admitted that it was a forward pass, but was unable to correct the call under the laws as they stood in 2007. This admission did little to pacify the New Zealand rugby public.

The suspicion that the French might be the All Blacks' World Cup kryptonite would linger until the ABs were able to put that particular dragon to the sword in 2011.

TOP 10
WAYS TO FEEL LIKE A MAN AGAIN AFTER THE ALL BLACKS LOSE

1. Get blind drunk.

2. Throw rocks at passing cars.

3. Body-slam the family pet.

4. Drive drunk.

5. Throw a pie at a homeless.

6. Take a shit in a policeman's hat.

7. Passionately kiss another man.

8. Push your feelings deep down inside so nobody knows they exist until they turn into an ulcer the size of a fist.

9. Ring up talkback and blame the loss on feminists, gays and foreigners.

10. Get over it and move on with your life.

Recreating this haka in the carpark of a pub while shitfaced is proven to raise your testosterone by 47 per cent.

5: Rugby World Cup: Suzie the waitress

'We were definitely affected, whether it was poison or bad luck. There was definitely something in the food.'—Colin Meads, All Blacks manager

WHAT HAPPENED: In 1995, the All Blacks' hopes of winning a second Rugby World Cup were high. Jonah Lomu had burst onto the scene, a burgeoning rugby colossus redefining the winger position and capping his ascension by destroying English fullback Mike Catt before scoring in a now iconic piece of rugby history. Expectations were high that Lomu's brilliance, coupled with a veteran squad featuring such all-time greats as Sean Fitzpatrick, Zinzan Brooke and Ian Jones, would help carry the ABs to glory.

Unfortunately, in the days leading up to the match, a bout of severe food-poisoning ran through the All Blacks squad. The tsunami of diarrhoea and vomit cancelled training sessions and felled the majority of players. After the game it would be suggested that the food poisoning was a deliberate act to cruel the All Blacks' chances. No proof was ever offered, but a mysterious waitress known only as 'Suzie' would be fingered as the culprit.

The resulting match was a tense tussle, a triumph of ten-man rugby as the Boks smothered the expansive All Blacks and forced the game into extra time as both teams failed to score a single try. The match would eventually be decided in South Africa's favour by a booming Joel Stransky drop-kick deep into extra time.

WHY IT'S SHIT: For the rest of the world, the Springboks' victory in the 1995 World Cup was a moment that transcended sport, when a fractured nation rose as one to celebrate a famous victory over an old foe, providing the famous image of recently elected president Nelson Mandela in a Springboks jersey hoisting the William Webb Ellis trophy—a saccharine Hollywood moment that was later turned into a saccharine Hollywood movie starring Matt Damon and Morgan Freeman. For All Blacks fans, the 1995 Rugby World Cup will always be remembered for Jonah Lomu smashing a bunch of Poms and a shifty waitress named Suzie and her dodgy tikka masala.

4: Team New Zealand blow 7–0 lead

WHAT HAPPENED: The 34th America's Cup in 2013 presented the best opportunity for Team New Zealand to reclaim the trophy since losing it to Alinghi a decade earlier. They began the competition strongly, defeating Luna Rossa in the Louis Vuitton Cup before squaring off against Oracle Team USA (run by old nemesis Russell Coutts) for the chance at reclaiming the Auld Mug for the first time since it was plundered by the Swiss. What followed was nothing short of a debacle.

At 7–0 up in a first-to-nine series, a Team New Zealand victory looked like a foregone conclusion. The champagne flutes were on the tables in yacht clubs and wankers' mansions around the country, awaiting the inevitable celebration. Yet, somehow, Oracle mounted the comeback of all comebacks to win eight races in a row to retain the Cup, consigning Team New Zealand's performance to forever feature on lists of 'greatest choke jobs in sporting history'.

WHY IT'S SHIT: Putting aside the obvious qualification that yachting isn't really a proper sport, Team New Zealand's diabolical 2013 challenge has a real claim to be the biggest sporting collapse in history. Perhaps the only thing that cushioned the blow was the fact that the average Kiwi understands more about the inner workings of a Gentle Annie than how an America's Cup race works—and cares even less.

3: The Underarm Incident

'The most disgusting incident I can recall in the history of cricket.'—Sir Robert Muldoon, NZ Prime Minister

WHAT HAPPENED: The third match of the five-match 1981 Benson & Hedges World Series Cup was an unlikely event to shape the sporting destinies of two nations, but the magic element of sport is its ability to surprise. The match was riddled with controversies—Martin Snedden claimed to catch Greg Chappell but was denied by the Australian umpires, who later failed to cover themselves in glory again when Richard Hadlee was given out LBW to a delivery blatantly pitching outside leg. The match earned its notorious reputation when Australian captain Greg Chappell instructed his brother Trevor to bowl an underarm delivery to number 11 Brian McKechnie to prevent him from hitting a six off the final ball to win the game. McKechnie responded by tossing his bat, in a now iconic image.

WHY IT'S SHIT: It would be impossible to discuss any list of the shittiest New Zealand sporting moments without including this quintessential event. The Underarm Incident involves all the classic elements of a shit sporting moment: blatant cheating, crushing defeat, and Australians. The incident was so shit that it has become synonymous with everything New Zealanders hate about our Ocker brethren: winning at all costs, breaking the rules, and not showing even the slightest bit of remorse.

2: The Springbok tour

'We won. We beat the protesters, we beat the media, and most important of all we beat the Springboks.'
—Ron Don, Auckland Rugby Football Union chairman

WHAT HAPPENED: In rugby terms, South Africa had long been New Zealand's nemesis, a legacy of brutal clashes between the two pre-eminent rugby nations forming a core part of the All Blacks legend. Unfortunately, the clashes had also been marred by the off-field controversy over South Africa's horrific apartheid regime.

In 1981, the Springboks' first tour of New Zealand since 1965 divided the country into two factions: pro-tour and anti-tour—those who felt that politics had no place in sport, and those who believed any sporting contact with South Africa condoned apartheid. Prime Minister Robert Muldoon, clearly a member of the pro-tour brigade, exhorted New Zealanders not to mix sport with politics, only a year after he had led a boycott of the Moscow Olympic Games to suck up to America.

As the tour moved around the country, the conflict played out between anti-tour protesters and the police, bringing the sort of violent disruption almost never before seen in this country.

WHY IT'S SHIT: Less a sporting event and more a political flashpoint for New Zealanders of a certain generation, the Springbok tour has become a byword for the sort of civil disturbance and social upheaval that seems almost impossible in New Zealand. It took a heady brew of the country's favourite pastimes (rugby and racism) to get people out in the streets, and over 30 years later 'the Springbok tour' still has the ability to inflame passions and make for awkward Christmas dinners.

The important thing was the ABs won the series.

1: Black Caps 'lose' World Cup final

'We never lost the game. We just didn't win it.'—Ian Smith, Black Cap

WHAT HAPPENED: After prevailing over a more-fancied Indian team in a bizarre 2019 World Cup semi-final played over two days due to rain delays, the Black Caps faced hosts and tournament favourites England at Lord's, the home of cricket.

Over the course of the tournament, the Kiwis had earned a reputation as plucky good guys countering their rivals with superior teamwork and commitment to playing the game the 'right way'. England, on the other hand, were filled with arrogant prima donnas and players they had nicked from other countries. Their only likable player was captain Eoin Morgan and they'd nicked him from the Irish. They'd even nicked their star player, all-rounder Ben Stokes, from New Zealand, and it's not like we have a surplus of quality cricketers just lying around ready to be nicked.[1]

The game was full of heartbreaking moments for Kiwi cricket fans. Lockie Ferguson's screamer of a catch to dismiss dangerman Eoin Morgan. Trent Boult catching Stokes on the boundary only to step on the rope. The ball ricocheting off Stokes' bat for four overthrows as he stretched out to make his ground. At the end of 50 overs the scores were all tied up, forcing the match into a Super Over, a contrivance

---

1   Stokes was guilty of the dual crimes of being a traitor and a ginger.

dreamed up to decide Mickey Mouse T20 games and now being used to decide the World Cup final. Even a Super Over wasn't enough to split the teams, with England and New Zealand scoring 15 runs each, setting the stage for one of the most absurd outcomes in the history of sport: England were awarded the trophy based on the number of boundaries that each team had scored in their innings.

WHY IT'S SHIT: It's hard to imagine a more brutal way to lose a World Cup—in any practical assessment the game was a tie and the only fair result would have been to share the title. The fact that it was decided by a means never used before only added salt to the wound.

A Super Over is a ridiculous way to decide a cricket game. Asking one team that has spent 50 overs in the field to come out and try to outscore a pair of set batsmen in a single over is blatantly stupid. The only thing dumber than deciding a match with a Super Over is deciding a match with a boundary countback. No sporting competition in the history of organised sport has been decided by a dumber rule.

It's a well-founded principle in organised sport that the winner is the team that scores the most points—awarding a winner based on who scored the most boundaries is a little bit like deciding an election based on who got better marks in year 10 home economics (which under MMP is actually a genuine possibility). The fact that a team that had built a reputation on fair play and upholding the spirit of the game was ultimately dudded out of a title by an obscure rule seems especially cruel.

The ICC recognised the absurdity of the outcome by promptly changing the rules and removing boundary countback as a means of deciding a game. New Zealand went on to lose in Super Overs three more times in the next seven months. Ben Stokes was nominated for New Zealander of the Year, which fortunately he didn't manage to win—nobody likes to see a happy ginger.

INDEX

First published in 2020

Image credits: Shutterstock (pages 2, 8, 11, 14, 17, 57, 58, 61), Unsplash (pages 13, 34, 73), Adobe Stock (pages 20, 80, 105, 120), Wikimedia (pages 39, 46, 97, 112), Kos Picture Source (page 42), Pxhere (pages 45, 109), Dave Lintott Photography (49 left and right, 93 right), Pixabay (page 65), Getty Images (page 86), National Library of New Zealand (pages 89, 101, 116), Photosport (page 93 left, 115 and cover)

Allen & Unwin
Level 2, 10 College Hill, Freemans Bay
Auckland 1011, New Zealand
Phone: (64 9) 377 3800
Email: auckland@allenandunwin.com
Web: www.allenandunwin.co.nz

83 Alexander Street
Crows Nest NSW 2065, Australia
Phone: (61 2) 8425 0100

A catalogue record for this book is available from the National Library of New Zealand.

ISBN 978 1 98854 762 6

Design by Kate Barraclough
Set in Sofia Pro
Printed in China by C & C Offset Printing Co., Ltd.

10 9 8 7 6 5 4 3 2 1